MW00962627

# MY
# EYES
## CAN SEE

Marcia,

May these quotes, stories &
reflective exercises allow your
eyes to see things differently
& give you NEW insight!

♡ Andrée Nice

xoxo.

# MY
# EYES
## CAN SEE

A YEAR OF REFLECTION AND INSIGHT

ANDRÉE NICOLE

Copyright © 2015 by Andrée Nicole.

| Library of Congress Control Number: | | 2014920528 |
|---|---|---|
| ISBN: | Hardcover | 978-1-5035-1769-1 |
| | Softcover | 978-1-5035-1770-7 |
| | eBook | 978-1-5035-1771-4 |

All rights reserved. No part of this book may be reproduced or transmitted in any form or by any means, electronic or mechanical, including photocopying, recording, or by any information storage and retrieval system, without permission in writing from the copyright owner.

Any people depicted in stock imagery provided by Thinkstock are models, and such images are being used for illustrative purposes only.
Certain stock imagery © Thinkstock.

This book was printed in the United States of America.

Rev. date: 01/13/2015

**To order additional copies of this book, contact:**
Xlibris
1-888-795-4274
www.Xlibris.com
Orders@Xlibris.com
672746

# CONTENTS

I wish to dedicate this book to my family, who showed me love while my healing was in progress.

Thank you, Wayne, for letting me be me even when my words, actions, and thoughts toward you were not very kind. You were patient and positive and chose to walk with me on this journey of *insight*.

Thank you for all the times you listened to my ideas and for the countless advice you've given me. But more importantly, thank you for allowing me to dream big and reach far beyond the stars. You told me that the skies were other people's limits, not mine.

I thank God for each and every one of my family members, my father, mother, son, and closest friends because they have all contributed in some way in shaping or forming what my eyes can FINALLY see.

———◈◈———

Each day my eyes can see more and more
as to which path I must take.

—Andrée Nicole

———◈◈———

# PROLOGUE

This is a GIFT to me, and having the opportunity to share *my story* has allowed me to experience a wealth of emotions—from fear to sadness, to frustration, to anger, to joy, and then . . . to happiness! More importantly, the concept of change and the beginning of a new journey presented itself to me, and because of these steps that were taken within these seasons, my eyes can see and I have gained a tremendous amount of INSIGHT.

# AS FAR AS EYE

# CAN SEE

# CHAPTER ONE

# A Journey of a Thousand Miles

———⟨❖⟩———

Courage is the journey that allows your soul
to go where there is no path for pain.

———⟨❖⟩———

When a person loses a job, ends a relationship, or battles an illness, the capacity to gain an accurate and deep intuitive understanding of these adverse effects may shake him to the core.

Making the decision to embrace the road you are currently traveling on or choosing to resist, react, and avoid the detours placed along your destination may drastically alter your path and cause you to wander to a desolate, unfamiliar place of paralysis instead of propelling you forward toward that place of self-growth.

I learned that this journey of impending change is probably one of the hardest places to be because the truth of the matter is that this change produces pain and exemplifies the ending of one's life and the beginning of another.

My change brought on confusion and mirrored a state of being constantly overwhelmed by the daily liberties of life. The journey of FEAR had set in and altered my perception of the things that I once perceived as simple. Now, they became rather mundane and complex, and the self-imposed limitations of my mind held me down, shackled me in bondage, and kept me as a prisoner. In doing so, the words that I now utter from my mouth have become cautious yet inspired to be spoken from a broken place that entertained the depths of my journey and my inner soul. A tender spirit silenced by trauma caused my single steps of physical, emotional, and spiritual well-being to become tainted, shattered, tampered with, and even unrecognizable to ME.

This change that I speak of happened in an instant, and normally, I would take the longer route home from work; however, on this particular day, I opted to avoid the late-afternoon traffic and therefore ended up traveling on a much less congested alternative route from the main road.

My journey ended with a thunderous clamor that jolted me in such an unexpected manner. This journey left an imprint on my mind, body, and spirit, and now my vehicle became tangled with another body of steel.

It took me a moment to digest the severity of what had just occurred. On that wretched day, both air bags became deployed and stung my entire face. This journey vehemently snapped my fragile head back against the car's headrest.

Vapors and strong odor began to seep in to the interior of the vehicle. It now adorned the traffic light pole that was situated on the curb of the sidewalk.

Clear fluids ran profusely from my nose, my entire body ached from shock, and now what used to be an empty street began to fill up rather quickly with witnesses to this tragic event.

My next journey began as I struggled with the opening of the vehicle door. After being unsuccessful with the third attempt, I began to panic, and for a quick moment, the thought of death entered my mind. However, on the fourth try, I was able to regain my composure and successfully exited. I stumbled over my own feet in total disbelief of what my eyes had witnessed and made my way toward the grassy area. I stood totally numb adjacent to where the accident took place and remain thankful to this day that my life had been spared.

The gentlemen that caused the accident, along with the other people present at the scene, gathered around me and poured onto the sidewalk. He asked me if I was okay, and I whispered to him that I was scared. I believe that seeing the traffic light dangling above the hood of my vehicle and also learning that because of this impact, the traffic light pole had caused the power outage in the surrounding area contributed to that feeling of despair.

That very morning, before I made my journey to work, my mother-in-law prayed for me and my son for our protection; she did not know that I would be a victim of a vehicular accident. I later learned that my father, on his journey home from work, had seen the very same ambulance pass by him on the street not too far from where I was located. He did not realize that it was en route to me. My cousins, on their journey home in the surrounding vicinity, spoke about me for ten minutes before I fell victim to this accident, an accident that would literally change my life forever.

To say the least, the pain and loss associated with this journey were frightening, and although some things remain a blur to me, the events and feeling associated with the police ambulance and hospital all seemed to be straight out of a movie and felt as if I were to be in *The Matrix*.

My life now consisted of attending weekly doctor's and specialist's appointments with physiotherapists, chiropractors, insurance companies, and adjusters to receiving acupuncture and massages, seeking MRIs, X-rays, CAT scans, to being drowned in countless documents and paperwork.

In response to this loss of control, I created barriers and mountains that ultimately blocked my ability to love and to care for others, even myself.

Anguish saturated my entire body without my permission, and I became emotionless and, therefore, delved deeper within myself until my voice became silenced. I came to the grim realization that I was no longer myself for anxiety and depression had taken over and I became paralyzed with FEAR.

Shortly thereafter, I had been diagnosed with posttraumatic stress syndrome. However, I remember that in the midst of uncertainty and chaos, another route had presented itself to me and allowed order to creep in.

Three weeks after, that journey would take yet another route. I began to let go and let my Creator be the lead pilot of my steps and slowly replaced the steps of fear with small steps of faith.

*A Journey of a Thousand Miles*

Reflection Response Exercises

Often, there are times when our paths may become altered. While we are on that path, we may encounter a few obstacles that present themselves when least expected. However, one must always remain focused and dedicated to the bigger picture in mind.

Remember that although you may not have been able to see it, those single steps and miles allowed this journey to happen and have made you that much of a stronger person today!

In the space provided below, begin writing down your own definition of the concept of journey. Upon doing so, think of a journey that has altered your way of life. It could have changed your way of being either physically, emotionally, mentally, or spiritually.

Then write down this journey that you encountered. Furthermore, share the single steps that you took and write about how you implemented these steps along the way of your journey. How have these steps contributed to where you are today?

_____

_____

_____

_____

_____

_____

_____

_____

# CHAPTER TWO

## Here I Stand

————⟨⊛⟩————

In the midst of your chaos, continue to
STAND for where there is no struggle,
there is no strength.

————⟨⊛⟩————

Human beings are simply fascinating creatures who not only have the power to stand outside of themselves but also have the ability to shape their own world from within.

A greater realization of the impossible often leads to many roadblocks in our journey of life. At about nine months old, babies begin to dabble into the world of discovery and begin to attempt to pull themselves up to a proper stance. Of course, with the help of an adult or some sort of furniture, often within a hand's reach, they are able to rise up to an upright position in order to stand.

The magnetism of becoming more autonomous when you are a child, a youth, or even an adult is regarded as a sense of accomplishment. Being able to be independent and provide yourself with all the things that you need to exist without having to ask anyone else for help is truly an insight to the human experience.

Replacing my steps of fear with steps of faith required a great amount of discipline and has not been as easy of a journey as I intended it to be. It felt like all the traffic signs and roadblocks led me to meander here and twist there without being able to locate the proper destination on time.

I had no inclination that the relentless intent and ferocity of these flairs of life lessons were taking an adverse effect on my well-being and were therefore affecting my ability to remain standing.

Now when I smiled, I smiled like nothing was wrong and spoke and acted like everything was perfect. I felt as if I were spinning out of control.

Problems began to surface and became magnified, and each insurmountable issue that arose now seemed to plague everything and everyone. And my efforts to rise to an upright position became more fruitless.

And then I began to crawl.

Things that used to give me great pleasure barely packed my interest these days, and I became unconcerned about everything. Expressing myself became a chore for me, food became the enemy, and to say the least, yelling became the only best form of communication. Then unwillingly, I began to withdraw myself further and further into a shell of despair.

One of the main issues that contributed to these episodes of isolation was my inability to stand.

In doing so, a void that needed to be filled could not be filled because of these unexplainable feelings of emptiness that I experienced every single second, minute, hour of the day, week, month of the year.

Painful physical and emotional memories associated with the motor vehicle accident stunted my growth to becoming the person I longed to be.

These sentiments of despair, anguish, confusion, and frustration paralyzed me, and I loathed them and often prayed that these feelings would disappear. I had been broken to the point where my independence had been shattered and prevented me from learning how to advance to the creeping stages of life.

I was *falling, falling* quickly out of love with my life and felt as if I were being sucked further and further into a black hole of agony that not only obstructed my will to smile but also interfered with my ability to breathe and stand.

Anxieties and depression seeped in to every pore of my body and remained there as an annoying, uninvited guest. I became despondent, uninterested and felt unloved despite the fact that I was surrounded by love. I detested who I had become and, more importantly, what became of my life.

I had become so numb that the light that struggled to remain bright grew dimmer and camouflaged my every being.

Yet in the midst of my continuous strife, my Creator became my source of strength and my rock.

I therefore blazed gloriously through my "new" life and remained extremely eager for action and was driven by desire to stand once more.

It took a great deal of courage, time, and effort on my part to pull myself toward a more confident and secure stance. Once this was discovered, the mountains of impossibilities began to be moved beyond my *faith* and the bridge over that troubled water began to be more recognizable.

For when I was unable to do anything else, I chose to stand, accept, and work through these life lessons.

*Here I Stand*

Reflection Response Exercises

For whatever reasons, there are times when you think and truly believe that you are all alone in the world and can no longer continue on with your journey because of all the challenges that presented itself to you on your way to healing.

Write about the time when you reached your boiling point and decided to just "stand."

When you made that conscious decision to stand in the midst of your trials and obstacles, what gave you the courage to stand in confidence that all would be well?

What suggestions would you give to others about how they should face their fears?

_____

_____

_____

_____

_____

_____

_____

_____

_____

## CHAPTER THREE

# A Season Of Faith's Perfection

———⟨⊹⟩———

Faith grows best in the winter of trial and
sings and dances ever so beautifully with CHANGE.

———⟨⊹⟩———

Some may describe a change in season as a subdivision of the year or as a significant difference in the weather, while others choose to identify this noticeable modification with the ecology of a particular hemisphere and the amount of hours of daylight in a given day.

All in all, these seasons are marked by changes and just as how the intensity of the sunlight—or lack thereof—would reach the Earth's surface. I too had experienced these shifts within the four seasons.

During the winter season, animals hibernate while the plants lie dormant. Similarly, I too distanced myself from the not-so-kind days that were often riddled with immeasurable challenges and therefore found refuge in the arms of nature.

In the midst of these challenges, I was able to succumb to an environment filled with constant motion, activity, noise, and even turmoil. It was during these times that I began to develop a deep appreciation for these seasons of faith's perfections.

The tree that stood outside my bedroom window became very symbolic to me in the sense that to the naked eye, one would sight our beauty. Just like the tree, others would see the trunk, bark, branches, and leaves, yet many would fail to realize that underneath the Earth are the roots that gave it life and sustenance.

The roots of this majestic tree represents my challenges, the constant rushing of thoughts, fears, anxieties, sleepless nights endured by physical and emotional pain.

*Winter*

In the midst of this chaos, winter had symbolized death and stagnation, and loved ones and friends chose to see what they could see, not realizing how misguided they had become about my changes, beauty, strength, and ability to cope.

Yet despite the darkness that was faced during these winter months, this season taught me the importance of faith, hope, and oneness. Perhaps it was the purity and freshness of the first snowfall that did it for me because when it snowed, all my cares and worries also became covered.

Snowstorms represent the trials and tribulations of my journey and remind me of the steps that I had taken; but more importantly, these steps had produced footprints that reminded me that I was never really ever alone.

They illustrated to me that my Creator has always been there with me, had never forsaken or left me, and would always remain by my side. And because of this, I am most grateful for this winter wonderland.

*Winter, Spring*

Spring represents rebirth, a blossoming into one's life or period of growth when things appear fresh, bright, and promising. For me, this season exemplified a time of new beginnings and balance, and I learned that in order to move forward, I could no longer focus on or be continuously preoccupied with taunting thoughts of the past.

Springtime cleaning was the most necessary procedure in order for complete healing to take place. Therefore, during this season, I focused on cleansing my inner self before any of the outer self could ever become an inward treasure.

*Winter, Spring, Summer*

Summertime, on the other hand, embodied a time full of joy and happiness, and I was finally able to relax and have some fun. This season denoted a time for my thoughts to be free and harmonized with life itself once more.

Despite the sweltering heat, summertime was a most joyous time for that was when I was at my best, when my health was most optimal and it showed.

*Winter, Spring, Summer, Fall*

Fall characterized yet another phase of the seasons of change, and while harvest took place and knowledge continued to form, the reality was that summer had come to an end and it was now time to focus.

Summertime had allowed my light to be rekindled and allowed me to get ready to fight the enemy that sought to keep me discouraged, disengaged, and depressed. I was set free, and my character had matured—and wisdom had been gained. I became more comfortable in welcoming this lifetime of learning for a sense of fulfillment had been bestowed upon me.

These seasons of faith's perfections have strengthened me and, furthermore, have allowed me to gain courage and persevere with any situation when the odds were stacked against me. I have often been told that there's a calm after the storm, and it is finally beginning to feel as if things are being knitted back together all in the name of restoration of my faith. I have grown, I have taken many risks, and change has presented itself in multiple forms in these seasons.

Looking back at my life within the last few years, I have endured the most treacherous journey that I have ever had.

All these seasons have perfected my faith in some way, shape, or form for it has allowed me to believe that there are new starts to everything, that from failure comes success and being able to experience optimal health is a gift.

CHANGE presents itself when least expected, but then restoration will come around full circle. This was a season of INSIGHT.

*A Season of Faith's Perfections*

Reflection Response Exercise

As human beings, we are rather impatient and would rather see speedy results. However, what we fail to comprehend is that the questions that we usually have are not always answered on our time. It is on our Heavenly Father's time. You had the opportunity to read about the importance of each season and what the various seasons signified for me. Now it is your time to think of your favorite season.

Begin with the end in mind and move toward creating a working definition of what that particular season may mean for you, of course, using your own words.

Now, commence writing about the steps chosen when having to let go and rely on your faith while you went through this particular season.

_____

_____

_____

_____

_____

_____

_____

_____

_____

_____

## CHAPTER FOUR

# I Am Rich

———⟨⊹⟩———

To be rich belongs to the definers,
not the defined; you are whole.

———⟨⊹⟩———

Many novels have been written on the subject of how to get rich. Even classes have been taught by people who have become rather convincing to those who are most eager to become successful millionaires in the shortest amount of time.

Not only have rich people devoted a lot of time developing other schemes enabling others how to successfully attain an abundance of valuable resources or material possessions but they also have informed these people that the accumulation of their wealth can either be attained through their careers, investments, or savings.

However, what they failed to tell these people is that getting rich is not as easy as many would have you believe. There tends to be one very important component to this life of luxury that many fall short of, and because of the lack of this, it therefore leaves people broke.

One Sunday morning, as I flipped through the channels, I stumbled upon an evangelist who spoke about whether or not people understood the true meaning of what it means to be rich. As I listened intently to the message that was being delivered, I questioned myself about whether or not I really understood what this phrase meant.

For me, the notion of being rich had already been established with the association and accumulation of wealth, not only within our society and community but within the world at large.

Although there is some truth to this belief, richness should not be defined by how grandiose your home is or by the kind of car you drive, nor should it be determined by the kind of brand-name clothes and/ or shoes you wear because you can have all these things and yet still be quite miserable, not to mention that you can also be broke.

Richness should be equated with one's inward treasure and being able to experience wholeness in every facet of one's life.

After I reflected about the true meaning of being rich, I rephrased the question that I had heard and then asked myself when the last time I felt completely whole, completely rich in my words, actions, thoughts, and more importantly, in my overall life was.

That was the moment when I became very intuitive and developed a deeper insight into these few powerful words.

For the longest while, I did not even recognize my brokenness. It was only when I was in the company of very close friends and loved ones did I learn about this void.

When I was broken, my words were broken, my thoughts were broken, my actions were broken, and I therefore behaved in a broken manner.

I detested every moment of it.

However, once I sought help. I was slowly guided back into the path of restoring my richness.

While on that path, I worked toward becoming healed, inspired, and strengthened not only in my mind and body but within my spirit as well.

In doing so, I became fully equipped with the necessary tools needed to nurture my rich treasures. And because of these rich journeys, I have grown comfortable in embracing and celebrating the prosperity and abundance of my own life experiences.

These rich episodes propelled me into the direction of taking on life's challenges with rich determination and rich drive.

*I Am Rich*

Reflective Response Exercise

Although this chapter is quite short, the message of being rich is quite enormous.

Think about what it means to be rich and then proceed to writing your own definition for this concept.

Also write about whether or not you are rich then document the reasons as to why and then create a plan to assist yourself on your journey to becoming and remaining rich.

_____

_____

_____

_____

_____

_____

_____

_____

_____

_____

_____

_____

## CHAPTER FIVE

# Refreshed, Renewed, and Restored!!

————◦❧◦————

Dancing with your obstacles allows you to
match the speed and rhythm of life with clarity
and restoration to self.

————◦❧◦————

As adults, we take many tests in the subject area of life just as how students take many exams throughout the academic school year. We can prepare ourselves for the upcoming tests by studying hours upon hours, or even days upon days, so that the final outcome may be rewarding both to the educator and the student.

Maturity is very much like taking a test in the sense that both require careful and thorough planning to reach an advanced stage. In doing so, one is able to face the truth without condemnation.

For such a very long time, I ran from the truth and questioned everything, which prevented me from advancing from a mental or emotional developmental level toward becoming complete.

My personality of always having things under control and getting the job done impaired my vision of what proper health and wellness should really look like.

Having many accolades attached to my person, unwillingly being placed on a pedestal by all family members, friends, and colleagues, was the norm for me.

After the traumatic experience of the motor vehicle accident, I thought that I could conduct myself in the same manner as before. However, when I was unable to continue on and perform my daily routines, I felt weary, behaved hostile, and became anxious. And in the midst of all these emotions, I still remained optimistic, thinking that I had everything under control. But because of my inability to recognize my failures, I struggled with maintaining adequate grades on the tests that were administered in the subject area of the restoration of life.

When asked by others if I was okay, my response to them was always "But of course I am." My rationalization for such a response stemmed from the belief that words sound powerful. If I were to speak using positive words directed toward my current situation, perhaps it would become a self-fulfilling prophecy where I would really be well.

Despite having to trudge through this mess, I faced the truth of my reality without any resistance of condemnation and became accepting of my brokenness and craved to be whole, to be rich, and to be ultimately free.

Now I fully understood the lessons behind these stories of sufferings. It would appear to the naked eye that because I was broken, I did not need to be invigorated by these trials and tribulations that were unnecessary. But I know that they all had been conveniently placed in my life to allow God to work within and through me.

This peace and energy that I speak of were further nurtured by visiting the house of the Lord for it had been some time that I had the opportunity to do so. Hearing the rhythmic beats of the instruments that were played that morning completed me. Hearing the angelic voice of the praise-and-worship team also spoke to every part of me for my spirit had been enthused. My spirit had whispered into my ear and spoke to me and embraced my yearning soul.

Then all the reservations I had about life became answered, and I was no longer afraid. And I began to critically assess the bigger picture to this art exhibit attached to me and titled *Life*.

Resuming, reestablishing, and having the ability to give freshness or strength to the things that I enjoyed became exhilarating again.

I became reinvigorated about life and had the energy to press on with my spiritual quest for oneness.

I was no longer just a student in the classroom. Now I was the student and the teacher, where at times I received a passing or failing grade in the subject area of grace. But in the end, not only did I become reacquainted with the ability to be free, to hope, and to excel, I finally began to see glimpses of me in a renewed, refreshed way that finally brought restoration to ME.

*Refreshed, Renewed, and Restored*

Reflective Response Exercise

Many people on a regular basis have to renew their passports, driver's licenses, or even library cards, for that matter.

One's thirst usually gets quenched after having a tall glass of raspberry lemonade filled with ice cubes during the scorching summer months. While that of the latter would work for me, another beverage of their personal choice may easily quench others' thirst.

One may also be physically restored by perhaps taking a well-deserved, candlelit bath filled with Epsom salt after a long day's work. All these illustrations speak to the concept of renewal, of being refreshed and restored.

Now it is your turn to think of a time when your cup was either overflowing or running empty. When did you realize that you needed to be renewed, refreshed, and restored? What did you do?

Let those creative juices flow and commence writing about that experience.

_____

_____

_____

_____

_____

_____

_____

_____

_____

_____

# CHAPTER SIX

# Love Is Like a Friendship Caught on Fire

————— ❖❖ —————

Conquer everything together with love
for infinity is before our eyes.

————— ❖❖ —————

Love remains to be the essential element in a person's life. However, in order for love to continue to survive, grow, and glow, one must be prepared for the peaks and valleys presented during these unions.

What many people tend to forget is that it is okay to have peaks and valleys in a relationship because it is a known fact that what goes up must also come down. When one climbs a mountain, they have to reach the peak of that mountain. Then once you have arrived at your destination, there is nowhere else to go but down toward the valley.

This process should never be looked upon or classified by others as being a disaster or that your relationship has failed and is therefore unsalvageable. Your relationship should be seen for what it is.

In doing so, one will realize the importance of that shift. That too is fine because it is preparing you and is also required of you to proceed to the next level.

Once you have accomplished this, your union will become even sweeter than before, and the gift of insight that you have attained while on that journey would have developed into a new, fond appreciation not only for yourself but also for your loved ones. You become transformed into a better listener and therefore find it easier to love endlessly.

Because of these insights to what people's eyes have seen and these infinite lessons about friendship, one will be allowed to fully comprehend the complexity of and the notion of the true meaning of love for it is neither here nor there but remains to be before a person's eyes.

The earlier childhood friendships that were developed with my father, mother, and brother are precious keepsakes that have equipped me with a shield of faith. This shield protected me during times of trouble and continued to do so when important milestones were being approached.

With my own eyes, I witnessed a phenomenal support system that clearly exemplified love, and although things sometimes became too overwhelming, the friendship always remained at the storefront and therefore became my source of strength.

There was never a situation that was too small or tall. It was quite evident that despite the relationship between the river flow and the cold mountain peaks, the unconditional love and friendship that flowed toward me never seemed to stop, which in turn taught me a great deal about how to be conscious and considerate of other people's feelings.

Embracing and celebrating these memories have allowed me to experience peace, joy, happiness, and how to love this spirit with this beautiful soul, my lover and my closest friend.

In the beginning, our love was like a flame, very pretty yet hot and fierce. There were the long drives, secret rendezvous, soft kisses, and countless gifts, love letters, and roses and the amazing conversations about how we would spend our lives with each other.

"Come walk with me, the best is yet to come." These words whispered to me by him allowed me to love him even more.

As time went on, you gave me a son—our promise from God. And I thank you because our son added yet another kind of love to the equation. A mother's love.

Throughout the years, it consisted of a few ups and downs; however, our love always remained as a light that has flickered relentlessly.

During the darkest moments and a time, when I was even a stranger to even myself, you showed me time and again that you would always be there for me. You were my rock, and alongside our Creator, you gave me an enormous amount of strength that allowed me to stand firm.

As our love grew older, our hearts matured, and our love became like coal, somewhat deep, burning, and unquenchable.

When you looked at me, your eyes would sparkle with an abundance of love and beam with the desire to protect. These moments have kept me energized and excited despite the fact that at one point, I had been unable to feel any type of emotion due to the brokenness that crept into every ounce and pore of my being. However, everything came full circle, and life became passionate once more.

Words cannot explain how much I love you. The way you make me feel, the touch of your hands, the warmth of your smile, and your words of encouragement have helped me in more ways than one.

These feelings that you have allowed me to feel have soothed my inner spirit and overwhelmed me with great joy.

You are my soul mate spiritually, physically, and emotionally. We have faced many challenges and have stood firm to each crisis, and now we have come out stronger than ever.

Our relationship is like a flame to fire for the flame has grown and continues to radiate heat and generate warmth each day more than before. And because of this, our love will always remain like a friendship caught on fire. I thank you for accepting me for who I am. I thank you for being by my side every step of the way.

Your love displayed to me that you would forever catch me whenever I would lose my stance. Your love has shown me that when I have cried, you have comforted me. And when I have laughed, you have always shared my joy.

That is why, my kindhearted spirit, I love you today, tomorrow, and forever.

# Love Is Like a Friendship Caught on Fire

Reflective Response Exercise

Our first real friendships are developed within our earlier years of life. Whether these relationships are established with your parents, relatives, or your teachers, they have all left an impression on your ability to create and sustain healthy comradeship. These relationships often helped me during my journey, and if it were not for them all, I do not know where I would be today.

Each relationship was unique in the sense that each had contributed in a way that equipped my inward treasures. In doing so, I was able to continue to move forward with my healing process. Love lifted me, and I am most appreciative of the love that surrounded and encircled me.

Your task is to think as far back into your childhood. Now think of the different types of relationships that you have had. What were the ones that stood out for you the most?

List the reasons as to why they had such a positive effect on you. Now think of a time when you needed them the most. How did they love you back to life? Explain.

_____

_____

_____

_____

_____

_____

_____

_____

# AS EYE SEE IT

# CHAPTER SEVEN

## Deepest Fear

―――――・◈・―――――

Life should not be feared;
it should only be understood.

―――――・◈・―――――

Some day it stormed so hard that drops of pain fell from my eyes. But as I learned to see beyond my fears, as I learned to face and release these fears, as I learned to hope, my vision cleared, and I began to see the joy that lay beyond the pain for these walls of resentment and mistrust began to melt down to a form beyond recognition.

The enemies of inadequacy and darkness that had at one point frightened me no longer served its purpose. I struggled with this forever, replacing my steps of fear with faith. It often felt like I was on a roller coaster that shifted to and fro from fear to faith to faith to fear and then back to faith.

I talked a good talk, yet when it was time for me to walk, I always seemed to become immobilized. I had to return to the classroom of persistence and constantly work to perfection or work as possibly close to getting to it.

I felt as if I were a marathon runner. The constant tests of endurance, fitness tests, and then more runs. Having to adjust to this new lifestyle was hard work, but then again, who said life would at all be easy? Like many athletes had discovered, the training and the hard work paid off.

I no longer felt as if I were shrinking beyond a form of nonexistence. I was no longer wrapped up in a state of depression, nor was I losing any more races. I was becoming a WINNER.

Those feelings of insecurity that had once rained on my parade, which had turned my clouds and skies to even more somber moments, miraculously changed into a brighter azure sunlit sky.

Once I decided to take that step, I leaned in to the wind and pushed. I pushed so hard that my deepest fears no longer prevented me from shining. There was no longer a resistance to dream because now I radiated rays of hope, resilience, strength, beauty, intelligence, and more importantly, LIBERATION.

Shackles no longer bound me. I was set free. Free to dream the impossible dream. I was free to be me.

My deepest fears taught me an invaluable lesson to fight even harder than I did before because I was meant to shine.

I worked feverishly day and night to develop my ideas so that it could manifest into a reality. The thoughts of my future and the numerous business endeavors that were dancing around my head almost became addicting to entertain. However, I realized that because of these addictions, I was allowed to act and create many programs very dear to my heart.

From my past experiences, I was able to bring a voice that was once silenced back to life. Once I let go and let God, everything fell into its rightful place. Beautiful things happened in my life when I distanced myself from my deepest fears. The realization of the latter no longer frightened me; it gave me sporadic bursts of energy and allowed me to keep moving far and beyond what my human eyes can see. I realized that I was getting higher and higher, closer and closer to my dreams that at times it almost felt surreal.

My deepest fears had become blessings, and my failures miraculously transformed into success. The only thing that I need to do now is to abstain from the pleasure of feeding myself with these negative thoughts and fears so that I may continue to gain vital benefits because fostering an environment of sensitivity would only encourage a climate of difficulty, which in turn would make the task of fulfilling any of my purposeful thoughts into a mere setback.

There is no looking back at this point of my journey for my eyes continue to see that sometimes our deepest fears are ourselves. We are our worst known enemy to self.

*Deepest Fear*

Reflective Response Exercise

Read over part of the poem titled "Our Deepest Fear" by Marianne Williamson provided for you below, and write your interpretation of these eloquent words.

What is your deepest fear, and how is it powerful beyond measure?

---

> Our deepest fear is not that we are inadequate. Our deepest fear is that we are powerful beyond measure. It is our light, not our darkness, that most frightens us. We ask ourselves, who am I to be brilliant gorgeous, talented and fabulous? Actually who are we not to be? You are a child of God. Your playing small doesn't serve the world.
>
> —Marianne Williamson

---

_____

_____

_____

_____

_____

_____

_____

# CHAPTER EIGHT

## Never Say Never

——❦——

It is deep as the ocean and high as the sky,
yet they remain your limits, not mine.

——❦——

Many people frequently ignore what their bodies are trying to tell them. Unlike those people, I choose to honor my body's request. However, this time, my "Spidey senses" choose not to cooperate the way in which they normally would have, like in the past.

All week, these outlandish feelings stirred up concerns of confusion for me. However, in the midst of this confusion, these foreign feelings remained accurate. They all pointed to these subtle clues that ultimately led me to the conclusion that something was not right.

Nonetheless, I continued on with my daily routines until the pain became totally unbearable. That is when the pain prompted me to visit the emergency section of the hospital.

I absolutely loathed hospitals—the smell of them, the long hours of having to wait to be seen by a physician. All these things absolutely MADE MY BLOOD BOIL. I could never imagine working in any of the medical facilities under such compromising conditions and circumstances every single day!

Being short staffed, having to deal with frustrated and annoyed patients, and attending to potential patients who at times seem to only clog up the common waiting area and hospital corridors must take its toll on them.

Just thinking about it contributed to my attitude being less than joyous. The reminder of having to sit on such uncomfortable chairs brought that reality closer to home, and now my body became more of an enemy rather than an ally for sitting on these chairs and seeing the rows and rows of people with cuts, bruises, and various kinds of illnesses coming to and fro became more and more depressing by the minute.

Strangely enough, everyone in the waiting room developed some sort of strange bond due to the long hours of having to wait (somewhat) patiently for your name to be called.

Funny enough, I would have chosen to be seated in that waiting room rather than having to prepare myself for the unforeseen news that I was about to receive.

Remaining cool under the circumstance was an understatement. Each step thereafter caused me such enormous pain. The difference in the way that I walked foreshadowed an event that I did not want to face.

This was devastating news. I was losing the baby to an ectopic pregnancy. I remember sitting in the doctor's office after the loss of our second child and feeling absolutely numb. A coldness filled the entire room that prevented me from even uttering a single word. Thereafter, the physician's words became a blur and were then reduced to an almost inaudible whisper.

All of a sudden, I heard a voice gently whispering in my ears that all is well, would be well, and to never say never. It was the oddest feeling one could ever experience because although we had just learned of our precious gift being lost, hearing that almost inaudible voice in the sterile room was rather comforting. A sense of relief came over me, and I exited that doctor's office and never entertained the conversations again.

I became pregnant a third and then a fourth time, only to experience devastating losses.

A part of my soul died that day, and it felt as if my heart had broken into a million and one pieces. I still yearned to be a mother to this precious gift that was given to be used and so quickly taken away.

My pregnancies evoked scores of mixed feelings and conjured up a plethora of questions about the possibilities and outcome of what could have, should have been.

Despite the roller coaster of emotions, I refused to allow my eyes to remain within the boundaries of fear.

Marvelous transformative processes had taken place within me. I had the opportunity to bring new life into this world, and although the pregnancies were not carried to full term, I remain holding on to those words of encouragement that were whispered into my ears that day—to never say never.

# Never Say Never

Reflective Response Exercise

You will never be able to accomplish that! Never do that again! Never put all your eggs into one basket. Have you heard of any of these sayings before? Well, what about the phrase "Never say never"? I am sure we all have heard these phrases at one point in our lives.

I would like you to think of a time when all odds were stacked against you. Now, try to recall if a particular person ever verbalized to you that an idea or dream you have had could not be attained.

How did this make you feel? What did you do? Did you allow these pessimistic thoughts, actions, or even words of others prevent you from getting what was rightfully yours?

Write about this time and what you did in order to combat the never-say-never syndrome.

_____

_____

_____

_____

_____

_____

_____

_____

_____

_____

# CHAPTER NINE

## It's Hard to Tell

---◆◆◆---

When we sail in the ocean,
we may occasionally drift.

---◆◆◆---

Getting back on track after you have taken an unexpected fall not only requires a lot of energy; it also requires a tremendous amount of courage on the person's part to take that initial step.

With some hindrance, I stepped out of my comfort zone, and then I leaned into the wind and pushed even harder than before. It is said that some people go through more pain and suffering than others, and I seemed to have regularly fallen into this category of grief.

The burden I carried paled in comparison to that of anything else that was going on in my life at that particular moment.

Many days I wished that I could have waved a magic wand and just make all the pain and suffering go away, but the reality of this was that I could not.

I had to deal with the initial shock of it all, all over again and again. The ugly reality of these episodes was that it was not just sadness.

I did not feel like a woman and felt like I failed my partner and myself. It was more than grief for the precious gift that no longer was a part of me. It was the constant replaying of those haunting words uttered with reluctance from the lab technician's mouth—it's hard to tell.

From that point forward, the ability to exercise patience was not at all easy. The reality is that we live in a time where messages and information can be sent across the world instantly and everything is available with only a few clicks of a mouse, and I had grown accustomed to living in this quick-fix world. Although not warranted, I expected my pain and suffering to be addressed and fixed instantaneously; why would I ever want to exercise patience?

I grew more impatient with each tragic event that had been attached to my person. I began to question whether or not things would ever be the same or at least within acceptable limits of some normalcy.

It was really hard to tell if being impatient, frustrated, angry, and sad were the only things that I was good at because it seemed that I had mastered these feelings with ease. They were all too familiar to me, and I wanted them to distance themselves from me and from my life for a long time.

It will always be hard to tell what life has predestined for us. We are people that like to grasp and attach ourselves to people, concepts, and things. Because of the pain and suffering that I had experienced, I was allowed to fully equip myself with an armor of patience. Time after time, I had waited in haste for my healing to take place, for the pain to stop, for the suffering to come to a halt.

Once I had understood the significance of time and the importance of its role, I realized that I do not have any control over the amount of time that is required when having to deal with these endless episodes of emptiness.

Patience is indeed a virtue that has shown itself to me that can be cultivated and nurtured over time; however, it was most difficult to let patience have its perfect way work within and through me.

## It's Hard to Tell

Reflective Response Exercise

Everyone wants to have a good life; no one wants to suffer. When you really think about it, has anyone lived a whole life without some measure of loss, grief, pain, or hardship?

Isn't it funny how things can be going great one minute and then, in the wink of an eye, the total opposite presents itself like an unannounced relative who now has shown up at your doorstep, telling you they are here to spend not one day but a month with you.

Although this may sound funny to some, it may be really annoying and unwelcoming to others. My question to you is what do you do in a situation that presents itself like the scenario that has just been illustrated? Do you welcome this unexpected visitor with open arms, or do you pray that the month will go quicker than you would expect it to and continuously grumble with complaints?

Think about a time when something that you had longed for, even hoped for, and prayed for showed up when least expected.

Write about how that had made you feel to know that your prayers had been answered. Now think of that something that you had longed for, even hoped for, and prayed for being no longer there.

What emotion did you experience, and how was it different than what you had felt before?

_____

_____

_____

_____

_____

_____

# CHAPTER TEN

## *Emotional Grind*

—————— ⋆⊰⊱⋆ ——————

Clear your mind of *can't* because you can.

—————— ⋆⊰⊱⋆ ——————

Being able to gracefully accept the twists and turns in one's life brimmed with an immense amount of impediments requires a great deal of determination. The ability to tolerate these interruptions made it rather grueling and resulted in more frustration, with I being easily agitated and upset most of the time.

The continuation of the panoply of emotions served as a springboard that led to deep reflection about what matters most and, secondly, the importance of remaining positive during a time of distress.

My family, health, and wellness will always be the most important things in my life. I can't imagine not having any of these sacred things in my immediate life for it would make this journey even harder than it already is.

The emotional grind that followed the miscarriages was heart wrenching, dreadful, and most draining. There will never be enough words to describe the feelings one go through when having to make the necessary adjustments to the required steps in preparations for that journey.

Despite the importance to move on and to acquire the admirable quality of patience, this advice did not help me to tolerate others nor lessen the gap between what I had and what I wanted without becoming upset. This was difficult for me to accomplish, and therefore, because this was known to me, these goals became loosened from my grip and became more unattainable with every grasp.

I told myself the biggest lie—that I could not do it—and therefore, I continued to experience emptiness until an internal switch brought me to the realization of the importance of remaining positive and, more importantly, accepting the things that throw themselves at you in this game called life.

It was then I began to accept rather than judge and resist *it*. Once I learned acceptance and being able to remain positive in challenging circumstances, I began to find peace within myself.

Being able to accept what things were, seeing those things more clearly, addressing the things that were being resented, and dealing with the things that needed to be changed illustrated to me that *nothing lasts forever.*

*Emotional Grind*

Reflective Response Exercise

Why do people have to experience such a sea of emotions? Wouldn't it be awesome if throughout our lives, you would only have to experience joy and happiness, not having to worry about the what if's or why did it have to be this way? Furthermore, having the opportunity to eradicate all traces of anguish hurt and pain? Wouldn't it be so ideal? Wouldn't it?

The truth of the matter is that we all know that we would never grow and would not gain any strength if our lives were only filled with the good times or positive experiences.

Despite how painful and foreign these emotions may be, we must learn to take the good with the bad and continue on with our emotional grind.

Having said that, I want you to think of a time that left you emotionally exhausted. Now, see if you are able to condense those thoughts into the format of an acrostic poem for the words *emotional grind.*

Remember that in order to create an acrostic poem, you should write the title (emotional grind) vertically on the page. In this case, there are fourteen letters in your title. Now get your poetic juices flowing!

_____

_____

_____

_____

_____

_____

_____

# CHAPTER ELEVEN

## Fistful of Tears

———◆◆———

Yesterday's pent-up tears will flow,
Heal, and educate you more each day.

———◆◆———

I became isolated even though I had plenty of emotional support for my feelings. I felt a sense of incompleteness, and therefore, I continued my quest in search for answers that, strangely enough, I already knew.

The intensity of my grieving process was like a large burning flame. In my case, the usual friends and family who would normally offer sympathy during such a time were absent because very few people knew of the pregnancy in the first place.

By not informing those who were within my circle of love, I was prevented from accepting the reality of the loss, which I learned the hard way to be a major component of the grieving process.

I found that I grieved more for the lost dreams of becoming a mother again. I cried and cried and then cried some more and then found myself turning more to alcohol to relieve the pain and suffering even more quickly rather than if I were to have dealt with it by myself.

Although in my heart I knew that this was not the proper thing to do when experiencing such a lost, I also knew that what I was doing became a Band-Aid solution. In my heart I knew that it was wrong. The rationalization for me was that I just wanted to feel numb even if it were just for a few minutes out of my wretched day.

The beginning stages, especially having to accept the reality of the loss of this precious gift then having to adjust to the new situation, brought on many heart-wrenching, crying episodes. It felt as if I were going insane. I know that my family did not enjoy seeing me having to go through this for it tore them up and affected them greatly in return. God knows that it was not my intention to torment any of my loved ones. This just hurt so badly.

This, therefore, encouraged me to resume my role and self-identity as it once was prior to becoming pregnant.

The fistful of tears were a fresh reminder that I am human and, more importantly, that it was okay to cry. These tears encouraged me to go to a place that conjured up a lot of pain. However, as many the tears that had been shed may have been, these fistful of tears had the power to break the chains of my injustices. They cleansed me by purging me from all the sorrow that had swollen my heart.

Crying, I learned, is never a sign of weakness—and I needed to fully understand this in order to not forget, but to heal, and more importantly, be delivered from this heavy burden of grief.

The fistful of tears allowed me to participate in the process of reflecting on my life on every level. In doing so, the latter encouraged me to value the importance of reinvesting my emotional energy in developing new relationships, building new ties, and lastly, nourishing the relationships already present in my life.

This needed to be done in order to reap the benefits of a healthy recovery in order to become whole once more. By making a step into the direction of acceptance, the power within me was ignited.

*Fistful of Tears*

Reflective Response Exercise

People cry for many reasons. It may be because they are extremely overjoyed, frightened, frustrated, sad, or even angry.

What are your reasons for crying, and what led you to this place of despair? Was it because you have witnessed your child experience heartache and wished that you could protect them but are unable to do so?

Or was it because of a coworker who inadvertently harasses you day in and day out? Or perhaps you cry because that one person in whom you confided in ultimately betrayed your trust?

Either way you look at it, we go through the motion, and sometimes more than other times, we have also shed fistful of tears. Take a moment to gather your thoughts then provide your written response to the kinds of emotions that were involved when you visited that place of despair?

_____

_____

_____

_____

_____

_____

_____

_____

_____

# CHAPTER TWELVE

## When It Rains

—— ❧ ——

Raindrops are heaven's tears.

—— ❧ ——

The lyrics to the song "Here Comes the Rain Again" composed by Annie Lennox came to mind as I sat at my dining room table that is situated in front of a gigantic window overlooking the main road. As I looked out this window, I noticed that the usual white clouds formulated by ice crystals had now become flattened out and reduced to mists of huge gray vapors. Yet as I looked out my window, the gloominess, coupled with the rain, provided me with some kind of comfort. In my pajamas, socks, and overly sized slippers, I felt some sort of peace being bestowed upon me.

For many, rain is seen as an annoyance than anything else. Many city dwellers cringe to know that the meteorologist has foreseen rain in their beloved forecast. When others complain, I embrace and celebrate it for they are my showers of blessings!

Rain is not only a source of nourishment for the Earth; water represents life. Whether it is in the form of a gentle sprinkle, light watering of the Earth, a torrid downpour, or flood, I absolutely love the rain!

As a child, I can remember clear as day walking through the rain and feeling refreshed. As an adult, I rarely use an umbrella, and while others become worried about getting their clothes soaked or their hair wet, I stroll in the rain and treat it as if it were to be a bright and sunny day.

Raindrops are heaven's tears. They represent my sorrow and my anger toward the events revolving around my losses. Therefore, when it rains, I feel cleansed and I smile because in my eyes it is a form of renewal and forgiveness.

It's a form of renewal for me in the sense that I am able to gently pick back up the pieces and, at my pace, carefully create and then complete this puzzle. I realized that I was my worst enemy and that I held myself hostage for something that I should not be made to feel accountable for. I needed to forgive myself for the way I treated ME. Ironically, the rain came at the most appropriate time for me that morning because I learned the importance of never giving up despite what may be thrown your pathway.

I continue on with my journey of life and travel down whatever path or wherever the road may want to lead me. Each step leads to a place of restoration and peace. I look forward to some normalcy in my life, where I am not subjected to having to wake up to a splitting headache because this pest usually remains with me, as if I needed a personal bodyguard until it is time for me to go back to bed. I long for some normalcy where I don't have to ride on an emotional roller coaster that dips and turns and places my world upside down.

*Toujour mes anges* best describes the eternal love I will have for my children, who have gone on to a better place. I know that I will see them one day. I also know that it will take some time for me to heal from every loss I have experienced in such a short space of time. However, through it all, I thank Mother Nature from the depths of my soul for nourishing the Earth with the downpour of blessings for the rain is so symbolic of my never-ending obstacles being weathered then washed away.

Therefore, the rain will forever be an inspiration to me and will always be a friendly reminder to me of the importance of rising up after any fall. Therefore, I continue to RISE.

*When It Rains*

Reflective Response Exercise

There are many slangs that are used among people and, furthermore, terms or phrases that I am sure you have heard of at one point in your life that revolves around the symbolic meaning of the water of life.

Perhaps you have heard the expression "Don't RAIN on my parade." When it is used in this context, rain is seen as a spoiler of a big event. I am also quite sure that you have also heard this before: "Save it for a RAINY day," which simply means that one is to save something good to brighten up a gloomy day. When there is a postponement or cancellation of an outdoor event because of rain, people would often use the phrase "RAIN out" to describe what has happened in the event of it raining. And lastly, when there is a very heavy downpour of rain, the idiom "It's RAINING cats and dogs" is usually used.

What I would like for you to do is to think about whether RAIN is seen as an annoyance or a blessing to you and explain how His water of life is symbolic to your life.

_____

_____

_____

_____

_____

_____

_____

_____

# EYE AM AWARE

## CHAPTER THIRTEEN

# Stars in the Sky

---◆◆◆---

Your beam of light will never grow dim,
only if you let it.

---◆◆◆---

The thought of spending Christmas in the Caribbean among family and friends sounded like the most sensible thing to do. It was like music to my ears.

Our parents had finally completed the construction of their other home in Jamaica, and now as a gift, they were inviting their children and grandchildren down for a time of fun, celebration, and more importantly, relaxation.

The idea of waking up to the warmth of the sun, seeing endless rows of palm trees and even parrots flying so freely in the azure clear skies sounded more enticing than waking up to frigid temperatures in a city submerged in several feet of snow. I love my country; however, the mere fact of having to commute in this weather to any destination via the well-slickened roads and having to walk on sidewalks glazed with ice, to say the least, did not tickle my fancy at all.

This mini vacation was very much needed for everyone, and I am most grateful that our parents went through great lengths to make this family reunion at Christmastime one of the best and most memorable ones for us all.

I welcomed this invite with open arms for I became extremely weary battling these storms consecutively, and now I had the opportunity to just rest. Rest my mind and body and become spiritually in tune with my Creator once again. It was so vital for all these things to be restored.

All the hustle and bustle involved in the preparation for when one travels can become extremely draining. However, those feelings quickly became eradicated once I had boarded the plane. Once seated, I exhaled. Exhaled all those pent-up feelings that took up occupancy in my mind, body, and spirit for so long, becoming released like the sweet fragrance of a flower.

As I sat within the confinements of the aircraft, fond memories of Jamaica and my visits as an infant, child, teenager, and young adult flooded my thoughts and instantaneously allowed me to feel *irie*. I always had great times with my grandparents, cousins, aunts, uncles, and friends and with my parents. Going on trips to the beach, visiting the countless tourist attractions, bartering at the straw market, climbing up Dunn's River Falls . . . the night life and the FOOD! Because of these memories, I will forever hold them in my heart and love my sweet, sweet Jamaica.

I must have dozed off for now I awakened to the thunderous claps of the occupants in the aircraft. We were now landing on the tarmac, and the excitement began to bubble up with anticipation about my meeting with a good friend named *restoration*. And now it began to overflow when I saw my parents.

I cannot begin to say how relaxed I began to feel. It was as if each layer of doubt, frustration, fear, deceit, and pain began to peel away down to the core of my being and I showed. My skin began to glow, my hair began to grow, and my mind began to become knitted back into one.

The feeling of not having to experience any form of anxiety and being able to keep my head afloat was a huge accomplishment, and I felt like a winner. The sounds, smell, sights, and tastes of Jamaica gave me great pleasure; however, I would have to say that the greatest pleasure was being among the stars.

Every night before turning in for bed, we would go outside into the crisp yet refreshing midnight air. It is still unfathomable to me how beautifully lit the skies were for it were as if our Creator got a jar full of stars and scattered them throughout the galaxy. There seemed to be more than one hundred million of these sparkling objects everywhere, every night, and to say the least, I was starstruck and often stood in awe of their incandescent presence.

We continued our rendezvous among the stars in the sky, accompanied by a stroll. Other nights we just sat on the front porch and talked about everything under the moon related to our dreams and the importance of restoration of one's health. These nights that I spent in the Caribbean, underneath the umbrella of magnificent stars, reintroduced the possibility of hope and faith to the things that once lost their luster for life.

I am thankful for these moments because in my adversity, I learned to be thankful even when things looked grim. Looking up into the sky and then seeing the stars brought things into greater perspective for me and reminded me that this florescent light was a path that became symbolic to my own vision. I was encouraged to see the galaxy—in this case, the bigger picture—interpret and ponder about everything and then synthesize it all in relation to my circumstances.

The stars in the sky allowed me to think about everything that was, and I became entailed within my frame of thought. In doing so, these endless thoughts allowed me to continue searching for that light that shone so bright in the darkest moments in my life.

*Stars in the Sky*

Reflective Response Exercise

Have you ever looked up into the sky at night? Perhaps it was during a warm summer's night when the meteorologists had said to take special note of the constellation of stars.

Or perhaps you were able to do so during the times when you and some friends went camping. Or maybe you were able to do it while taking a stroll along the boardwalk with some friends who were visiting the city.

Either way, you have had the opportunity to look up into the sky, although the visibility of the stars in the sky would be most clearly seen by the naked eye in the countryside as opposed to the city.

How did you feel when you participated in stargazing? What were your experiences when you looked up into the sky?

Write about that time when you were able to reach beyond the stars.

How was this act symbolic of reaching those higher heights?

_____

_____

_____

_____

_____

_____

_____

_____

# CHAPTER FOURTEEN

## *His Hands*

---·❦·---

Infinite love evokes new thoughts of expression.

---·❦·---

There are many different kinds of therapy or remedies that have been used by people throughout the world, each carefully crafted to help people cope with and eventually eliminate some of the unwanted fears.

Many of these treatments have been rather successful while others have not. The ones that have been usually aim to equip the person with the necessary tools they would need to take care of their inward treasures.

Interestingly enough, the counseling was very insightful and allowed me to really delve into areas that I simply had no answers to. In spite of this successful outcome of self-analysis, it was the mere simplicity of a slight touch and the holding of my hands that gave me comfort and ultimately nurtured and healed me back to life.

I usually am unable to return to my slumber sometimes for up to four hours at a time. It was during these times when the turbulent sea of emotions decided to fiercely sweep me up and carry me far beyond the comfort of the seashore. When this usually happened, I would utter the word *babe,* and out from beneath the comforters and bed linens, outstretched are these hands—his hands. It was our language. A form of communication that incorporated a touch from him that allowed me to feel safe and secure.

In my times of need, his hands represented the epitome of strength. He was my shield, and he protected me from these unwanted feelings that seemed to enjoy invading my privacy in the dead of night, when all I really wanted to do was sleep and be at peace.

I love him even more because he allowed these feelings to slowly dissipate by simply placing his enormous fingers in between my petite fingers, allowing our hands to be locked in love without uttering one word of solitude. His concerns, his love and caring gestures spoke volumes to me and will continue to do so until my prayers for guidance, strength, and direction are answered from my Heavenly Father.

The warmth that emanated from these healing hands was unfathomable to me for not only did it allow me to quickly escape from the reality of loss but I was able to fill that void and visit a land filled with an abundance of peace as well.

*His Hands*

Reflective Response Exercise

There are many studies about the numerous benefits of people being held after undergoing traumatic experience in their lives—whether it is a newborn baby who has been recently placed in the neonatal intensive care unit in the labor and delivery ward or an elderly person who has been placed in a home for adult living.

Everyone requires a dose of affection. For some, it could be the stroking of one's cheek while for me, it is the simple act of my hubby holding my hands. When he holds my hands, all my anxieties and worrisome thoughts dissipate.

Think of a time when someone held your hand. Write about that time and then describe the feeling you felt when the hand-holding event took place.

_____

_____

_____

_____

_____

_____

_____

_____

_____

_____

## CHAPTER FIFTEEN

# Adore You

---◈◈---

My heart is held in your hands,
and yours in mine, for a lifetime.

---◈◈---

It just feels like yesterday when this child was born. My son, who is now twelve years old, is growing quicker and getting more handsome with each passing year. He has grown into a tween who continues to possess the winning traits of determination, dedication, intelligence, and charm.

His name tells a story and depicts who he truly is. God is gracious to have chosen us for him as parents, and as a token of appreciation for such a glorious title, we cherish him every single second of the day by showing our undying, eternal love for our son.

Every parent will boast and say that their child is the most adorable one. However, when I speak of how beautiful this child was and is, I speak only the truth.

He was a baby with a head full of curly black hair who had a cool complexion. From his pudgy little fingers and toes, his fresh baby scent to his infectious smile, topped with his old soul, he left many utterly speechless and in awe of his beauty.

I was the proudest mother on Earth when he was born, and I continue to be extremely proud to hold this title. Our role as parents never ceases to stop and requires a lot of time and energy for you continually love, pray, care, and worry for your children endlessly. When our son was young, he was sickly, and although he had a crib, he spent most of his time in our bed. Watching him sleep was an absolute treat, and therefore, these moments that have been stored in my memory will be cherished forever.

I could watch him for hours and would often do just that. I would watch him until I become so fatigued that I would end up surrendering to this extreme measure of exhaustion. Then I would cuddle up with my son, legs outstretched and free from any form or trace of chaos from the precious hours.

These moments are just some of the illustrations of the first real relationship that my child would have developed with me as his parent. We have developed many special bonds. He has made me laugh, cry, proud, has driven me crazy, but more importantly, my child has seen me fall, cheered me up, and kept me going. And because of this, my dear son, you have taught me that no matter how old I get, I will always adore you.

*Adore You*

Reflective Response Exercise

Parents, aunts, uncles, or grandparents would agree at some point that children are blessings who bring joys and excitement to the life of others.

Whether your experiences of excitement are categorized as positive or negative, many would conclude that children are adorable precious gifts.

Think about a child who you adore. Now write about the most memorable moment you had with this child.

_____

_____

_____

_____

_____

_____

_____

_____

_____

_____

_____

_____

_____

## CHAPTER SIXTEEN

# Orchids

---◈◈---

In the landscape of beauty and strength,
the fields blossom with insight.

---◈◈---

I have always appreciated nature for its magnificent and splendid beauty, especially flowers. I don't think that there is one flower that I do not admire. However, besides totally appreciating the essence of a rose, I would have to say that I love everything about orchids.

I became so intrigued with this piece of natural art that at one point, I wanted to have it tattooed on my body. However, I decided that I would not proceed with this thought until I was 100 percent sure. For now, it continues to be admired from afar, in magazines or gardens for that matter, and perhaps when the time is right, I will revisit this thought.

What I love most about the orchid is its poise and its mere exemplification of true elegance, refinement, and innocence.

I find that no matter what challenges I am faced with in my life, I always try to look on the brighter side of things and see how I may learn from these challenges. Usually, the lessons to be learned are far more meaningful than any television program or lecture for that matter. In extension to these aha moments, I find that I am always able to make connections to that moment, to that object, to that person, to that article—basically to anything.

Funny enough, my son always says if there is never a time that I am not able to make connections with myself, the world, or other pieces of text. In response to my son's question, my answer still remains no. I am just beginning to realize why orchids are the most highly coveted ornamental plants to me. It is no secret that I have gone through a lot! It is most definitely a season of INSIGHT that has been filled with unforgettable events riddled with wisdom.

After having done some research, I found out that these exotic and graceful flowers also represent me for I too represent love, luxury, beauty, and strength. I too, like these orchids, convey pure affection and represent mature charm. I did not always feel that I represented these fine qualities; however, being determined to not let these mountains define who I am allowed me to transform into a field of magnificent orchids.

My mother recently told me that she thought that she was strong and continued to say that I am one of the strongest women that she knows and that I truly exemplify strength. The funny thing is that I am only mirroring her. For years I always saw my mother as a woman who wore many hats, who always had such great poise, elegance, and strength. I thank her, along with so many others that have instilled this beautiful attribute.

*Orchids*

Reflective Response Exercise

If you could use a flower to explain or describe your strengths and inward treasures, what flower would you chose to illustrate you and why?

_____

_____

_____

_____

_____

_____

_____

_____

_____

_____

_____

_____

_____

_____

# CHAPTER SEVENTEEN

## *This Moment*

---·❧·---

Listen to the still sounds of the water for
each drop requires you to hear.

---·❧·---

Warm, candlelit bathes allows me to abandon my worldly roles and step outside my structured life. It is a time void of the daily expectations present in my life. These moments have been allotted for me and only me to enjoy the sounds of the mere water splashing feverishly to cover my entire body.

The flickering of these lights that illuminate on the walls dances to and fro to their own beat and allows me to sink physically and reflectively into a world that promotes inner growth.

Most of these "spa moments" spent in the bathtub were especially reserved for most of my thoughts, dreams, and intermittent fears. Interestingly enough, these thoughts that had many questions produced answers in the depths of these waters for it was here that this moment reminded me how deprived I had become.

The idea of a new territory that I so eagerly wanted to discover allowed my creative juices to flow abundantly. They inspired me to try something creative and new, something rested upon my heart for a very long time.

This is the moment when all things pointed to the direction of within. The idea constantly presented itself to me during the late-night hours.

You see, it has been exactly a year that a vision to empower others was implanted deep within my soul. After I watched a segment from a television program, the initial stages of my business plans began to unfold. A purposeful name was crafted up, and the commencing of the mission statement, vision, and values of my business had been tailored to perfection. It seemed as if everything else was or had already fallen into their rightful places and at the appropriate time.

The website colors, photographs, programs, and all the workshops that would be offered, the business cards, were meticulously planned. I honestly believe that being an educator and having to wear many hats within this profession further assisted me to finally make this decision to leave the teaching field.

I will always be a teacher and continue to be an outlet for others so they too may have the opportunity to reach beyond the stars. Issues that revolve around children, youth, and women will continue to be a part of me.

My desire to give back to the community and the society at large has rested heavily upon my heart. I want other women to learn, be inspired, and then equip themselves with a voice that speaks victory.

To those long nights I am most thankful for because it was during these moments when my organization, Rich Chicks, was birthed.

The moment of casting all fears aside and trusting the unknown, that this was the most perfect decision to follow through with and make into a reality, was finally here.

Rich Chicks exemplifies the epitome of health and wellness. It speaks of healing, educating, inspiring, and equipping women's inward treasure. Rich Chicks will also enable people to come together and will empower women to magnify their voices that had once been a silenced dialogue.

*This Moment*

Reflective Response Exercise

When is it ever the right time to make that initial step? When will "this moment" ever be the perfect time to step out from your comfort zone and celebrate the unknown?

At one point in your life, you have thought about those questions and have also probably heard the harsh responses from other people, telling you that you have worked extremely hard to get to where you are now and that you should reconsider wanting to make any types of changes in your life.

But sometimes, you just want a bit more, so does that make it okay to throw everything that you worked hard for all away?

These are some of the dilemmas that many people face on a regular basis. However, some people do honor their gut feelings and throw everything away for happiness.

Think about a time when you had to make an important decision and had to abandon all of society's expectations. How did you feel, and did you experience any resistance once you chose to follow your heart's desires?

Now, write about how your beliefs and dreams allowed you to succeed.

_____

_____

_____

_____

_____

_____

## CHAPTER EIGHTEEN

# In My Zone

---·❦·---

Time left alone in the wilderness requires you to
think about your thinking and reveals the truth.

---·❦·---

Valuing the importance of taking care of yourself is a win-win situation
any way you look at it because everyone knows that commitments can
take a toll on you especially if you are not careful. The responsibilities one
may have might have the tendency to pull you in countless directions,
which in turn can make you feel stressed out, short tempered, and
overwhelmed.

It cannot be stressed enough—the importance of finding the
rhythm between all the roles that one may have to juggle. Playing your
deck of cards right will ultimately result in a healthier family and, of
course, a healthier you. So that's why today I chose to wake up not
wanting to do anything!

As gross or irresponsible as it may seem, I did not want to take a
shower, make breakfast, see anyone out the door, tell anyone to have a
good day, or even clean up the house. All I wanted to do was just lie in
bed, wrapped up in my gargantuan comforter. I decided that I would

watch some television programs when I wanted to and have a bite to eat if I deemed it necessary to do so.

Not wanting to speak to anyone nor wanting anyone to speak to me seemed like the best solution at the time because at least I would not be forced to explain the reasons for this silenced dialogue.

Being in my zone felt exhilarating, and opting to not have my cell phone on or within hand's reach is highly recommended for everyone to have on their to-do list. I felt as if I were no longer a hostage to this communicative world because my world consisted of making and answering calls, texting, and sending messages via my cell phone, Twitter, Hotmail, Gmail or Facebook accounts. Having the opportunity to purge myself from this addictive behavior and from all this technology made me even more of a fugitive from the social media world.

Not having to answer to anyone allowed me to take a time out from the craziness that comfortably took occupancy in my life. Once I took this time out for myself, I came to the realization that I have become overwhelmed with my life.

A small request from anyone or having to tackle new responsibilities was more than I could govern. And for that reason, the time for self-care preoccupied every pore of my body.

I needed to be refueled in order to give back to the well-being of myself. In doing so, the needs of everyone else would be fulfilled only when my own emotional and spiritual cup became refilled.

Who would have thought that having one day, just one day, to fully experience being void of anyone or anything and having the ability to bask in my zone would result in such important life lessons? I have learned that life isn't an easy journey. Everyone has their own journey, with their own wants and needs.

Being in my zone taught me that I must understand and embrace life although it may throw many loops my way. Being in my zone allowed me to celebrate those loops and be fully charged and ready to face them. This was a step in the right direction and the recipe needed for my optimal health.

*In My Zone*

Reflective Response Exercise

Being alone with your thoughts is not necessarily a negative thing. The nature of one's thoughts and individuality is the heart of self-realization. When one abandons their worldly role and commences to step outside that structure, an insight of truth normally reveals itself. This is normally referred to as being in your own zone.

Think about a time when you were in a zone. How did you get there?

How did these obstacles lead to these moments of self-realization?

_____

_____

_____

_____

_____

_____

_____

_____

_____

_____

_____

_____

_____

# CHAPTER NINETEEN

## Awaken

---·⬥·---

Sometimes you have to gently brush
away the cobwebs of yesterdays.

---·⬥·---

These tears that flow from my eyes and trickle down the side of my cheeks do not come from a place of fear or sadness but comes from a place of knowing that I am a spiritual being having a human experience.

I am fully aware that truth can stir something up within the depths of your soul because I am a living testimony of this. I finally experienced that emotional lift that I longed to feel.

After spending most of my time judging and limiting myself with the past experiences riddle with fear, tragedy, and loss, I understood that I had settled into an "I can't" consciousness that at the time seemed completely logical, although I knew better that this thought process or rationalization was wrong.

To say the least, the difficult is easy; the impossible took a long time. But in the midst of this journey, something happened!

Once more I became awakened to the idea that there is always a depth potential of strength within us even in times of weakness. While experiencing these moments of darkness, my Creator continued to guide me and love me through it even more, and it was because of His grace I arose from my slumber.

I began to see clearly to the beliefs that ran in my life. I no longer questioned who I was, and I had the ability to decipher the difference between pure awareness and what I was aware of before I could see with clarity as opposed to remaining confused, unclear, and having a multitude of questions that I did not know the answers to. My desire to become more spiritual allowed me to spiritually grow and concentrate on being just me. In doing so, naturally I began to unfold and split any boulders that would obstruct my growth.

I began to listen to my emotions and observed my true self and, in the process of doing so, sought me. I was no longer stuck in a particular mode of suffering and became more alert to whatever that would arise. My ability to expand beyond my normal boundaries or laws of perception motivated me to begin to practice for self.

Moving to the next stage on the awareness continuum had cancelled every plot, plan, and scheme of fear that tried to prevail.

I became awakened to who I am as a person. Awakened to the necessary steps required to make my dreams a reality, which in turn left me feeling happier and more relaxed. I had more energy, and therefore, I was able to let go of the tendency to try to achieve oneness because the reality is I AM ONE and have always been.

I also let go of trying to achieve healing because I now know that I AM WHOLE and have been awakened to wonder once more.

*Awaken*

Reflective Response Exercise

A single event can awaken us. These events are neither written on paper, for things written on paper can be erased, nor is it etched in stone, for stone can be broken. But it is inscribed on our hearts, and there it shall remain forever.

So what should one do when encountered with stillness? Do we embrace this silence and then celebrate the thoughts and ideas that came from them, or should we remain in a spiritual slumber?

One thing that is quite clear to me is that without change, something sleeps. Think about a time when you were physically, emotionally, mentally, and spiritually fatigued.

During those moments of distress, was it easy or difficult for you to awaken once you were asleep?

Write about a time when you were spiritually awakened. What led to this experience, and where are you now because of this awakening?

_____

_____

_____

_____

_____

_____

_____

_____

_____

## CHAPTER TWENTY

# The Promise

————⋅❧⋅————

Deceit enslaves while honesty liberates one from self.

————⋅❧⋅————

I have told you time and time, again and again that you are no longer a best friend of mine, and you are definitely NOT welcomed here! Do you not see that your words, your actions, and your thoughts attempted to paralyze my dreams, my desires, and my destiny?

Can you not understand that you have only caused a tremendous amount of pain, discomfort, confusion, and heartache? Or did you think that your kind gestures were doing me more of a favor than of the harm you forced upon me?

Nonchalantly, you silenced my voice. You silenced me, talking like you had my best interests in mind. Lies, lies, and more lies infested every pore and ounce of my mind, body, and soul. Very crafty PAST! However, what you failed to realize is that I am and have always been a CHILD OF GOD!

*Excellent, omniscient, omnipotent, loving* are the words that best describe my Creator—my Jehovah Jirah—for he picked me up from the pits of hell, from the MIRY CLAY.

Reflecting upon the trials and tribulations of the past few years evokes a sea of emotions.

Anxieties, animosity, and the many sleepless nights—all these things, including the losses, no longer haunt me, no longer stifles me, and no longer steals my joy. You thought that because we were best friends, our friendship would last forever, that we would be inseparable. However, there is a time to cry and a time to laugh, a time to mourn and a time to dance.

My deepest fear was that I would become comfortable with not having that light that shone ever so bright and, furthermore, that it would remain and be known to others and, more importantly, to myself as just a mere flicker of despair and destruction and defeat.

However, with the help of my blessed Savior and my beloved family and friends, I began to reach again, this time, well beyond the stars.

I realized that you, my ex-best friend, that the skies may be your limit. But they absolutely do not define me or what I am capable of becoming or where I am destined to go. They are not mine.

These seasons of faith's perfections have allowed me to evolve and experience these journeys and accept them humbly for what they represent. I have stood firm, I have become refreshed, renewed, and restored. I have become RICH and have experienced love to last me a lifetime.

Today, I celebrate MY promise and begin to record yet another chapter in my book titled LIFE. As I approach each day, I am reminded by my journeys, that I must continue to honor my mind, body, and soul.

From this day forth and for eternal sake, I will remember the importance of the immense power that my words, thoughts, and actions bring forth.

Magnificently, I have realized that these words can alter one's mind, body, and soul in a positive or negative manner.

However, with the guidance of and blessings from my beloved Creator, He has guided me to this spiritual path and led me on a journey of a thousand miles. And these experiences, these lessons have given me the strength and refuge that I required in my times of need.

By allowing myself to continue experiencing these single steps of sweet union, friendship, respect, perseverance, joy, peace, happiness, and love with myself and loved ones, I know that I will continue to practice the essence of faithfulness. And in doing so, I will continue to share these memorable moments of what I have learned so that I may inspire others to use the tools they require in order to equip their inward treasures because my past does not live here anymore.

*The Promise*

Reflective Responsive Exercise

Normally, people make promises to other people about things they hold dear to their hearts. Sometimes, these promises are kept, while in other instances, they have been unfortunately broken.

Despite the inconsistencies of keeping a promise, would you not say that the best gift that anyone could ever give to themselves is a promise?

According to Hannah Arendt, "Promises are the uniquely human way of ordering the future, making it predictable and reliable to the extent that it is humanly possible."

Think of something that you would like to have had accomplished. It can be on the larger spectrum or even on a smaller scale.

What will your gift or promise be to yourself? What are the steps required to accomplish this goal or for it to take place?

_____

_____

_____

_____

_____

_____

_____

_____

_____

_____

Edwards Brothers Malloy
Thorofare, NJ  USA
March 27, 2015